Save our girls

Female Genital Mutilation:

The Cut That Imprisoned Our Bodies in Pain

By

Martha w. Alday

Table of Contents

INTRODUCTION

Female genital mutilation (FGM), also referred to as female circumcision or female genital cutting, is a painful, degrading, and often fatal procedure that girls and women must endure in some societies. A portion of the genitalia is cut off using unsanitary tools and without anesthesia (FGC). The practice of FGM is held on by centuries of custom, culture, and incorrect ideas while being supported by poor literacy rates, the position of women, as well as insufficient access to healthcare facilities. This horrific act is anchored on the prevalent views of gender, power, sexuality, and identity. Women who have had FGM are highly regarded in places where it is practiced. In contrast, those who have not had the procedure are thought to be immature, unaccepted by society, rejected by the neighborhood, and unfit for marriage and parenthood. The likelihood of becoming a social pariah, rejection by peers and family, and loss of stability and support are some of the powerful motivational reasons that predominate in practicing societies. In a patriarchal culture where women lack autonomy, power, position, and education,

Marriage is the primary means of survival and security. Those who uphold it defend it, saying that the day of circumcision is a celebration of success as it marks her entry into womanhood thus promoting the idea of early marriage. While keeping in mind the effects of change on mothers' self-esteem, it is critical to recognize and safeguard the needs of girls who have not yet undergone circumcision when addressing the challenges of FGM.

CHAPTER 1

Many years have passed; although outlawed in most areas highly practiced, the excruciating pain sowed in the bodies of more than a 100million girls subjected to this horrific procedure still lingers. FGM(Female genital mutilation), a supposed gift every mum is to pass on to every girl child she bore, intending to prepare and guide her through the journey of womanhood and motherhood, turns into a nightmare and will be passed on for generations. The Bodies of our Mothers, Sisters, Cousins, Aunts, and Friends were modified, Rights infringed upon, and forcefully, the pleasure we embodied was snatched, and pain took its place forever. Grab a seat, and let's talk FGM

MEANING OF FGM

All practices that entail the partial or complete removal of the external genitalia or other harm to the female genital organs (such as sewing the labia majora or pricking the clitoris) for non-medical purposes are known as female genital mutilation (FGM). FGM obstructs typical bodily processes and offers no health advantages.

Here the female genitalia is modified, cut, or harmed on purpose. Traditional practitioners carry out this procedure with little or no knowledge of human anatomy or medicine, utilizing unsterile instruments and in unhygienic settings that create opportunities for significant health issues. The phrase "mutilation" emphasizes how seriously this practice infringes on the rights of women and girls. This word also stresses the seriousness and severity of the act, clearly distinguishing it from male circumcision. It is ideal not to use the phrase "female circumcision" because it implies the same thing as "male circumcision" and leads to misunderstanding. The assumption that FGM is safer when medicalized has led to an increased engagement of healthcare professionals in this operation. FGM is seen as a violation of girls and women's human rights on a global scale. It severely discriminates against girls and women and violates children's rights since it almost always involves minors. There are societal, religious, and cultural justifications for the practice.

CHAPTER 2

THE BEGINNING OF FGM(ORIGIN/HISTORY)

Multiple hypotheses swirl around how Female Genital Cutting (FGC) came to be, even if the precise cause of its beginning is unknown owing to the lack of sufficient evidence. FGM predates Islam and Christianity, although some groups claim it is a religious need. Patriarchal social structures and traditional group or community cultures tend to implement them. There seems to be a connection between slavery and FGM. The finding of circumcised mummies from the fifth century BC has led some scholars to suggest that it originated in Ancient Egypt, which includes modern-day Sudan and Egypt. In a quest for slaves, Egyptian kings expanded their realm to include the southern area. As a result, slaves from Sudan were transported to Egypt and the adjacent region. This explains why it is referred to as "Sudanese circumcision" in Egypt and "Pharaonic circumcisions" (i.e., Egyptian) in Sudan. Infibulation and female circumcision was also exercised by the Egyptians to prevent conception in both women and slaves, making slave women with patched vaginas in great demand.

Other academics propose that the practice may have expanded along the lines of the slave trade from the Red Sea's western shore to parts of southern and west Africa, or it may have traveled from the Middle East to Africa via Arab traders.

International organizations, including the United Nations and the World Health Organization, are alerted to the health effects of female circumcision by African campaigners and medical professionals (WHO)

The International Day Against Female Genital Mutilation is on February 6.

CHAPTER 3

FGM CLASSIFICATIONS

FGM is performed by an older woman in the community, such as a relative or a traditional birth attendant. It is done without anesthesia, analgesics, aseptic methods, or antibiotics, all using specialized knives, scissors, scalpels, bits of glass, or razor blades. Girls' legs are bound together to keep them immobile for 10 to 14 days, promoting the development of scar tissue. The procedure is commonly referred to as "cutting" or "getting cut" by women who have had it done. FGM comes in a variety of forms and degrees of severity. Depending on the region and primary motivation for the procedure. It is carried out on women at various ages, including the first week of life, throughout infancy, before puberty, before the first delivery, and multiple times in the woman's life.

1. Type I (CLIDECRECTOMY): Removal of whole or part of the clitoral glans (the external and visible part of the clitoris, which is the most erogenous part of the female genital) and the clitoral hood (the fold of skin surrounding the clitoral glans). Subcategories of Type I FGM:

- **Type Ia:** Only the prepuce/clitoral hood is removed.
- **Type Ib:** Removal the clitoral glans with the prepuce/Clitoral hood.

2. Type II (EXCISION): Partial or complete removal of the clitoral glans and labia minora (the inner folds of the vulva), with or without removal of the labia majora (the outer folds of skin of the vulva). Subcategories of Type II FGM include;

- **Type IIa:** Only the labia minora is removed.
- **Type IIb:** Partial or complete removal of the clitoral glans and the labia minora (prepuce/clitoral hood may be affected).
- **Type IIc:** partial or complete excision of the clitoral glans, labia minora, and labia majora (perhaps affecting the prepuce/clitoral hood).

3. Type III (INFIBULATION): Narrowing of the vaginal opening with the formation of a covering that is created by cutting and realignment of the labia minora or labia majora.

The cover of the vaginal opening is done with or without the clitoral prepuce/clitoral hood and glans intact (Type I FGM). Subcategories of Type III FGM variant:

- **Type IIIa:** The labia minora is taken out and repositioned
- **Type IIIb:** Labia majora is taken out and repositioned

4. TYPE IV: All additional damaging practices to the female genitalia performed for non-medical reasons, such as pricking, piercing, incising, scraping, and cauterization, are classified under Type IV.

Reasons For The Practice Of FGM

Female genital mutilation signifies ingrained gender inequity in every community where it is practiced—supported equally by men and women, typically without hesitation.

And so, anybody who deviates from the norm risks rejection, harassment, and exclusion.

Families will find it challenging to stop the practice without assistance from the larger community. Since the perceived social benefits of the procedure are preached louder than its drawbacks, this increases the chances of this act being executed even when it is known to cause severe damage to females. The very purpose of removing clitoral tissue denies women the sensation of sexual power and responsibility. FGM is practiced nearly universally and unchallenged in some societies.

1. **Respect For Tradition**: FGM is seen as a component of the community's historical and cultural traditions. Women in the community often participate in and support thc tradition because they regard it as a way to show respect for the community's elders. Culture and tradition must never be used to justify violence against individuals, whether male or female, as they serve as a foundation for human well-being. Additionally, culture is dynamic and constantly evolving. However, efforts to end FGM should be devised to consider the communities' cultural and social history.

2. **The Rites Of Passage:** FGM is a significant rite of passage for girls into adulthood in many cultures. A ceremony or celebration is frequently held to commemorate the occasion. It could be seen as essential to becoming a respectable adult lady.

3. **A Social Convention:** Where FGM is often practiced, it is regarded as such. In contrast to those who do, people who do not follow the practice could experience judgment, harassment, and isolation from their communities.

4. **Enhance Fertility:** Men and women in certain societies that practice this belief feel that if a woman is not cut, she will not be able to conceive or may experience complications giving birth.

5. **Ensure Virginity, Chasity, and Faithfulness**: FGM is thought to protect a girl's or woman's virginity before marriage and to guarantee loyalty after marriage. Families may thus believe that FGM defends a girl's honor and that of her family.

6. **Cleanliness And Beauty:** In certain cultures, FGM is used to make females more aesthetically pleasing and "clean." Cleanliness can apply to the body—cut or closed female genitalia are occasionally viewed as more sanitary and attractive—but it can also mean spiritual purity.

7. **Marriageability:** Men are frequently expected only to wed women who have undergone FGM. In some circumstances, the practice may be sustained by the need and pressure to be married and the potential financial and social stability that marriage may bring.

8. **Religion:** Even though FGM is not addressed in important religious writings, some societies consider it necessary, and some religious authorities may even advocate for it.

9. **Femininity:** It is believed that removing the clitoris and other genitally male genitalia makes girls appear more respectable, feminine, and attractive.

However, these justifications do not counteract the harmful impacts of FGM, nor do any moral, medical, or religious motives concerning this blatantly patriarchal practice. It is merely extreme child abuse and exists only to undermine a woman's sexual liberty, as shown in the complete or partial removal of the clitoris, which is exceptionally erogenous for females. The clitoris is homologous to the male glans' and can too be removed if you will. Only the foreskin is removed during male circumcision, and is not in any way a component of the male glans. FGM frequently includes the removal of both the inner and outer labia. Due to conditioning to accept this as the norm, women, and girls who have had FGM may not even be aware that their vagina looks different than anybody else's or that their cutting is "wrong."

Medicalization of FGM

This creates a sense of false security. All types of FGM, including medicalized FGM, have significant dangers. Furthermore, FGM has no medical rationale. From the standpoints of public health and human rights, it is unacceptable to advocate for cutting or harming a girl or woman's genitalia and to recommend that a medical professional do so. Medical professionals that perform FGM falsely justify the procedure as safe or advantageous for the health of girls and women. Additionally, it may further institutionalize the practice because medical professionals occupy positions of authority, respect, and influence in society.

CHAPTER 4

THE AFTERMATH OF FGM

The results of FGM depend on various variables, including the kind done, the practitioner's experience, the hygienic settings in which it is conducted, the degree of resistance, and the girl's or woman's overall health. All forms of FGM have the potential for complications, but infibulation presents the most significant risk.

1. HOW DOES FGM IMPACT WOMEN'S AND GIRLS' HEALTH?

FGM has detrimental effects on women's and girls' sexual and reproductive health.

i) Immediate And Short-term Physical Health Complications Of FGM

- **Excruciating Pain And Tissue Damage**: Due to its extensive nerve supply, the clitoris and surrounding genital tissues are especially sensitive. FGM is typically done without anesthesia, which results in excruciating agony.

- **Severe Hemorrhage Can Result In Anemia:** Excision of the clitoris may include severing the clitoral artery, which contains blood flowing under high pressure and might cause bleeding. Blood vessels are also harmed when the labia are cut. Bleeding typically happens during or right afterward following the surgery.

- **Hemorrhagic Shock:** Haemorrhagic shock happens when insufficient blood flows through the body due to significant bleeding. Excessive blood loss may result with FGM because the genital tissues are severely damaged. •

- **Infection And Septicaemia:** Infection may happen if FGM is performed in an unhygienic setting using crude equipment, if there is a lack of sufficient wound care following the process or if the patient does not receive adequate treatment on time.

- **Swelling Of Vaginal Tissues:** Genital tissues are cut and damaged, which results in a localized inflammatory reaction. An acute genital infection can also result in genital edema.
- **Severe Urination Retention:** A local inflammatory reaction is brought on by cutting and harming the genital tissues.

ii) Long-term Complications include;

- **Difficulties During Childbirth:** Because the vaginal hole is too narrow to accommodate a baby's passage, many women additionally need to undergo another cut during childbirth. Women who underwent FGM will have a much higher risk of needing a Caesarean section, an episiotomy, a lengthy hospital stay, and experiencing postpartum hemorrhage than women who had not experienced FGM.

Further, prolonged and difficult labor can occasionally end in obstetric fistula and fetal mortality. The risk of a baby dying at delivery is higher among moms who have undergone more extreme types of FGM.

- When women are sliced open on the first night of marriage (either by the husband or a circumciser) so that the husband can be intimate with his wife, it might cause **Dyspareunia**(painful sexual interaction), which results in sexual dysfunction.

- **The dangers of HIV transmission** are high in communities where large numbers of girls are cut on the same day as part of a socio-cultural ceremony using one blade

Gynecological and urogynecological difficulties and illnesses resulting from FGM Includes:

- **chronic vulvar pain**

- **clitoral neuroma**

- **reproductive tract infections**

• menstrual problems such as dysmenorrhoea (painful menstruation) and difficulty in passing menstrual blood

• urinary tract infections, often recurrent

• painful or difficult urination

• epidermal inclusion cysts and keloids in the genital area

2. FGM'S PSYCHOLOGICAL IMPACT

i) Mental Health And FGM

Genital cutting may be a terrible experience for girls and women who suffer FGM, leaving a lasting psychological scar and negatively affecting their mental health. Specifically:

- **Anxiety conditions**
- **Post-traumatic stress syndrome (PTSD)**
- **Depression**

The discomfort, shock, and use of physical force by those conducting FGM can also result in psychological damage.

ii) Women who have had FGM may also experience **Chronic Pain Syndrome,** increasing the risk of depression, poor social functioning, worthlessness, guilt, and even suicidal thoughts, alongside other chronic pain conditions.

iii) Relations With Family: Long-term effects of childhood trauma might include "behavioral abnormalities and possibly loss of trust and faith in caregivers who have allowed or participated in a painful and upsetting operation." FGM "may be deeply ingrained in the child's psyche and may precipitate behavioral issues" The women spoke of experiencing extreme terror,

iv) Relationship with the Spouse: Painful sex, low levels of sexual satisfaction, and low levels of desire can all contribute to sexual phobia. Lack of sexual pleasure may cause a couple to become unhappy and could likely lead to husbands having adulterous affairs with non-FGM women. Additionally, a woman unable to engage in sexual activity may not be able to fulfill her function as a mother, which plays a significant role in some cultures. In certain cultures, the inability to have children is blamed on women and sometimes seen as a curse.

As a result, the woman may experience rejection from her spouse and extended family, leading to "further social isolation."

- **Deinfibulation:** Deinfibulation is a surgical surgery that opens up the closed genital scar tissue in a girl or woman who has undergone type III FGM to reverse infibulation. It is important to allow intercourse, make delivery easier, and improve health and well-being. Deinfibulation should always be performed before an episiotomy.
- **Re-infibulation:** A process in which a woman's vaginal aperture is made smaller again after being deinfibulated. It's often done after delivery. Medical professionals never advise re-infibulation. It is a pointless and uncomfortable operation.

CHAPTER 5

FEMININE SEXUAL RESPONSE

A woman's body and brain undergo several changes during sexual arousal and activity, collectively called the female sexual response. Initial explanations used a linear model with four stages:

Sexual desire,

Sexual arousal,

Orgasm,

Resolution.

In more recent years, this model has changed to consider the notion that not all women go through all four phases. For instance, a woman may not feel sexual desire but still choose to have sex with her spouse or partner to feel emotionally connected to them. Alternatively, a woman may feel sexual arousal and satisfaction but not climax. The integration of biological and psychological aspects into female sexuality is considered in more recent theories of the female sexual response.

These consist of: a sense of physical, emotional, and relational contentment/attraction, sexual stimulation, arousal, and sexual pleasure. More importantly, a woman must learn how to "listen" to her body to detect her sexual reaction and requires enough time to experience these biological responses for them to develop into pleasurable excitement; each woman has her unique pace.

Erogenous Zones of The Vulva

1) Labia Majora: during sexual excitement, the labia majora experiences congestion, which increases local sensitivity.

2). Labia Minora: During sexual excitation, these little folds of skin that are dense with nerve endings and blood arteries also experience substantial swelling, which increases sensitivity.

3). Clitoris: The clitoris is an organ below the pubic symphysis. Its purpose is to provide the woman with sexual pleasure. The clitoris has both exterior and internal anatomical features.

- The clitoral hood and the anterior fold of the labia minora partially or completely conceal the external (visible) portion of the clitoris, called the **clitoral glans.** Erectile tissue and many free nerve endings may be seen in the clitoral glans (twice as many as in the male glans). The clitoral glans engorges and becomes more sensitive during sexual desire.

- The **"body"** and the **"crura,"** which comprise the **clitoris' internal portion,** are positioned inside the female body. The crura contains erectile tissue. The vestibular bulbs are in touch with the crura and surround both sides of the vaginal entrance. The crura and the bulbs both enlarge and become more sensitive during sexual desire.

FGM solely affects the clitoral glans, the exterior (visible) portion of the clitoris. Under the scar, the crura and a part of the clitoris' body are still there.

Positive Outcome Of a Healthy Sexual Life

It is everyone's right to embrace, express, and enjoy their sexuality.

1. A person's sexual health and life satisfaction are intertwined and can have either a favorable or negative impact on one another.
2. Attachment and sexual activity are inextricably linked because of the hormones generated during sexual activity, which fosters a close relationship between partners.
3. Both men and women can experience less stress by having sexual relations and sharing love and desire.
4. Women who have had FGM dealt with a procedure that harmed the anatomical component directly related to the female sex response. This may have an impact on a woman's sexual health and happiness.

Sexual Immorality Should Be Treated As A Binary Problem

Most heterosexual sexual actions always involve two participants (occurs in binary form) with mutual consent. Therefore, both sides must work together to ultimately achieve the goal of eradicating sexual immorality in heterosexual settings—

which is undoubtedly a significant contributing factor to this horrifying act. The sexual lives of men and women will benefit when if the gender sex gap is considered. When women's sexual rights continue to be violated, as has always been the case, the whole image of sexual objectification of women becomes a determining factor as we are full-fledged beings and not simply a collection of flesh and bones. So we should be able to exercise their rights in matters involving their bodies.

1 Every woman and man has the right to live a sexually fulfilling life and to express themselves in healthy ways.

2 All women, cut or uncut, might be interested in their bodies and want to be handled and have intimate experiences. These emotions are normal and healthy. Having had FGM does not preclude a woman from feeling emotions or from expressing them.

3 With the proper assistance and care, FGM survivors who have trouble with their sexuality, can learn to lead satisfying sexual lives.

4 With time and experience, a person's sexual experience develops and changes. Many things may be studied and practiced to help one's sexual health.

The optimum environment will certainly be created for optimized sexual performance, whether for pleasure or childbearing, and this will put an end to societal and cultural structures that have allowed women to be sexually repressed.

CHAPTER 6

SUPPORT AND CARE FOR WOMEN AND GIRLS WHO RECEIVE FGM

1. Basic Communication Skills

- Establish a friendly atmosphere and refrain from pressuring any women or girls to discuss their FGM experiences.
- Use proper terminology and wording.
- At all times, ensure discretion and secrecy.
- Allow her to talk and pay rapt attention when doing so

2. Support and Care For Sexual Health

- Educate people on sexual health and sexuality to dispel falsehoods and negative ideas that keep them from engaging in healthy sexual interactions.
- Information about how to handle medical disorders that have an impact on sexual well-being

- Counsel the victims to help overcome the negative feelings they may have created towards their genitalia and promote positive views about sexuality.

3. Support For Mental Health.

- Educating and informing persons seeking or receiving mental health care will help them better understand and manage mental health issues.

- Reduce whatever existing stress that might lead to mental health issues; these are more severe in women dealing with other types of stress, particularly those connected to immigrating to a new country (3), such as unemployment, social isolation, poverty, and a loss of control.

- Enhance adaptive coping as it could be challenging for a girl or woman to resume her regular habits. Encourage her to make tiny improvements, especially in areas she previously enjoyed thus enhancing performance in everyday tasks.

- strengthen social support for women and girls who feel ashamed or guilty, especially if they have been exposed to people in the local community who have unfavorable opinions about them

Signs That A Girl May Have Recently Had FGM

• She has trouble standing, sitting, and walking.

• She takes longer than usual to urinate and has trouble doing so.

• She experiences recurrent or unexpected bladder or menstrual issues.

• She exhibits altered mood or behavior when she returns to school after a protracted absence (e.g., she is withdrawn or depressed).

• She is especially hesitant to get routine medical exams.

• Due to shame or fear, she has asked for assistance or counseling but hasn't been open about

Indications A Girl May Be At Risk Of Fgm

• She or a sibling requests your assistance; a parent or other family member warns you that FGM may be performed on the girl; or the girl discloses that she will undergo a "special operation," be "recognized as a lady," or "become like my sister or mother."

• There is knowledge or suspicion of a forced union. In addition, if the girl is from a community where FGM is still commonly practiced, it is also essential to address the risk of FGM.

• Attempts to engage the girl in health and welfare services (such as attending appointments) have repeatedly failed, or the girl's mother is adamantly opposed to her having a genital exam.

• She gets taken out of class to take a long break, or she mentions going on a trip—either overseas or to her family's town, where FGM is common—in the future.

Her mother, father, or both come from an ethnic community where FGM is practiced.

• The girl, her family, or her close friends bring up FGM in a discussion.

• Her mother, sister, or cousin about the same age have been cut.

• Her parents hold opinions in favor of the practice.

• If a woman who just gave birth (or her husband or another family member) asks to be re-infibulated after childbirth, her infant, if a female, may also be in danger of FGM.

What Can We Do To Put A Stop To Fgm?

Unfortunately, there isn't just one way to stop FGM. The procedure is tricky, and different things happen worldwide for other reasons.

1. Spread Awareness: Events like today's International Day of Zero Tolerance for FGM is an excellent way to do this. You may do this by bringing up the topic and initiating a dialogue with your friends or family, or you can use the hashtag #EndFGM/C to disseminate information on social media.

2. Become Familiar with the Warning Signs and Symptoms: FGM is a widespread problem forbidden in most nations. Therefore, becoming familiar with the symptoms and indicators may be helpful if you ever come across someone who is at risk of FGM. Examples of warning signs and symptoms are shown below:

- A girl "becomes a lady" or gets "readied for marriage" during a specific event or ceremony.
- Unexpected or protracted departure from school by a female.
- A girl struggles at school to stay up.

3. FGM Safeguarding Education: Providing your team or school with FGM safeguarding education is a specific action you can do if you work with children or vulnerable individuals. Keeping everyone in the group or institution aware can prevent abuse against children, and vulnerable individuals can be prevented.

4. Incorporate Men into The Discussion: FGM is performed to regulate women's sexuality, a patriarchal practice.

Even if this is true, many males in communities who practice it don't understand why women go through this process and accept it as "custom." Men should participate in the discussion for this specific reason. One of the organizations attempting to engage men in dialogue about FGM **is "Men End FGM".** Think about helping them by discussing FGM with a male in your life.

5. Support and Fund Activists on the Front Lines: The people on the ground preventing children and women from undergoing FGM are the unsung heroes of the struggle to abolish this practice. Frontline activists are responsible for endless numbers of people's protection and education as a group. The minimum we could do is provide them with funding and assistance. You may accomplish this by liking and sharing their content on social media. With the cooperation of the older generations, change the traditions: "Grandmothers used to narrate fables and fairy tales that had hidden life lessons. Similarly, grandparents were the ones who taught their grandchildren about sexuality. Young women should be informed about their right to control their bodies.

4. Discuss the Dangers and Reality of FGM: FGM has long-lasting physical and psychological on women and girls effects that must be acknowledged to stop girls and women from suffering in silence.

CHAPTER 7

FGM AND THE LAW

The worldwide policy agenda now focuses on ending female genital mutilation (FGM).

Recognizing the numerous human rights that FGM infringes, numerous Nations have passed national legislation that renders the practice illegal and consequently punished by law. While some nations have passed laws explicitly prohibiting FGM, others utilize laws against assault or child abuse to make FGM a crime. Additionally, a component of UN Sustainable Development Goal 5 aims to "eradicate all harmful practices, such as child early and coerced marriage and female genital mutilation" to promote gender equality and empower all women and girls. The World Health Organization estimates that more than 200 million girls and women have been subjected to FGM globally, with almost three million children at risk each year before becoming 15 years old.

FGM VIOLATES A SERIES OF HUMAN RIGHTS PRINCIPLES, NORMS, AND STANDARDS OF EQUALITY AND NON-DISCRIMINATION BASED ON SEthe

- Right to life (when the procedure results in death)
- Right to freedom from torture or cruel, inhuman, or degrading treatment or punishment
- Rights of the child.

Because it interferes with healthy genital tissue in the absence of medical necessity and can lead to severe consequences to a woman's physical and mental health, FGM violates a person's right to the highest attainable standard of health.

The Importance Of FGM Laws

There should be legislation that prohibits FGM for the reasons listed below.

- Laws that address FGM assist healthcare professionals in defending their objections to the practice and provide them with a valid justification for refusing the treatment, even when asked ito.

- Laws can deter individuals who want to continue the practice and result in abandonment when combined with culturally relevant education and public awareness-raising effort.

- Legal sanctions aid those who have given up the habit or want to do so, as well as their family.

- Nations that approve put into effect and respect FGM-related laws demonstrate their commitment to ending thc practice and upholding the human rights of women and girls.

- At the local level, the legislation reminds girls, women, and families of their legal protection against FGM and their right to bodily integrity. Girls and women must be safeguarded from FGM regardless of whether a nation has legislation prohibiting it, even in regions where it is regarded as a culturally important custom.

Conversing With Your Clients About The Law

Not all patients will be aware of the legislation concerning FGM. During medical consultation, health care professionals and respected community members can use the occasion to spread knowledge about FGM and any laws that are in place to protect girls and women from it. They can also advise patients and their families about the repercussions of breaking these laws.

Conclusion

FGM must be treated with the utmost care because it is ingrained in many Africans' cultures and seen as essential to their sense of self. African communities and foreign aid organizations must collaborate at the local level to assess the effects of the practice if FGM is to be eliminated. Women's empowerment is crucial for its abolition since it exudes gender injustice. The human rights of girls and women are brought to light when FGM is addressed via education. Eradication strategies based on educational rights provide communities with a variety of possible solutions.

www.ingramcontent.com/pod-product-compliance
Lightning Source LLC
La Vergne TN
LVHW020527160826
845677LV00015B/3949
* 9 7 9 8 8 4 7 9 8 5 6 3 5 *